one mince = 50 dinners

This edition published in 2012
LOVE FOOD is an imprint of Parragon Books Ltd

Parragon
Queen Street House
4 Queen Street
Bath BA1 1HE, UK

www.parragon.com/lovefood

ISBN: 978-1-4454-9512-5

Printed in China

Written by Linda Doeser
Internal design by Simon Levy
Internal photography by Clive Bozzard-Hill
Internal home economy by Valerie Barrett
Cover photography by Clive Streeter

Notes for the Reader
This book uses both metric and imperial measurements. Follow the same
units of measurement throughout; do not mix metric and imperial. All
spoon measurements are level: teaspoons are assumed to be 5 ml, and
tablespoons are assumed to be 15 ml. Unless otherwise stated, milk is
assumed to be full fat, eggs and individual vegetables are medium, and
pepper is freshly ground black pepper. Unless otherwise stated, all root
vegetables should be washed in plain water and peeled prior to using.

Garnishes, decorations and serving suggestions are all optional and not
necessarily included in the recipe ingredients or method.

The times given are an approximate guide only. Preparation times differ
according to the techniques used by different people and the cooking
times may also vary from those given. Optional ingredients, variations or
serving suggestions have not been included in the time calculations.

Recipes using raw or very lightly cooked eggs should be avoided by
infants, the elderly, pregnant women, convalescents and anyone suffering
from an illness. Pregnant and breastfeeding women are advised to avoid
eating peanuts and peanut products. Sufferers from nut allergies should
be aware that some of the ready-made ingredients used in the recipes in
this book may contain nuts. Always check the packaging before use.

Contents

Introduction

One of the best things about minced beef is its versatility. It goes with a vast range of ingredients to create a wide variety of different meals from burgers to pasta sauces and from stuffed vegetables to pastry turnovers. Its most immediately obvious partners are onions and garlic and, perhaps, tomatoes, mushrooms and herbs, but it responds to a multitude of flavours and textures, whether hot or aromatic spices, peas and beans, many kinds of cheese, a huge array of vegetables and lots of ready-made sauces and condiments, from soy sauce to mustard. Perhaps surprisingly, it even combines well with fruit, such as apples and raisins.

As a general rule, the basic mince mix (see page 8) works in one of two ways. The raw ingredients can be mixed together until thoroughly combined and then shaped into meatballs, burgers, kebabs, croquettes, pie fillings or meatloaf before cooking. Alternatively, the various ingredients can be cooked in a saucepan or casserole so that the flavours mingle deliciously for pasta sauces, braises, stews, curries, gratins and even soups. The endless variations mean that mince will never be used in the same way again – you can impress your family and friends with traditional favourites or try something different.

Quality & Economy

Minced beef is undoubtedly an economical choice for family meals, not least because a little can go a long way. This is especially true when it is combined with other ingredients, such as breadcrumbs, to make meatballs or burgers, or when it is served with plenty of filling carbohydrate, such as pasta or a mashed potato topping. It is easy to cook – in the following pages there are 50 easy-to-follow tasty recipes for all occasions – and it is popular with adults and children alike.

However, the quality of minced beef can vary widely and buying the cheapest you can find may often prove to be a false economy. Many supermarkets sell 'bargain' packs and although the meat may look perfectly satisfactory, it usually contains quite a high percentage of fat. Not only is this less healthy, it is also wasteful. In the long run, meat labelled 'premium' or minced steak is a better and more economical choice. Minced steak from a good local butcher is probably the best choice of all.

Supermarkets will often have special offers on beef mince, and you can certainly make savings on this versatile ingredient. However, it doesn't keep for long in the refrigerator, but raw meat can be frozen for up to three months. Many cooked dishes, such as Bolognese sauce, also freeze well, so batch cooking is a good way to save both money and time.

When buying fresh beef mince, check the use-by date and make sure that the pack isn't damaged and is properly sealed. Store on a low shelf in the refrigerator, away from cooked foods and ingredients intended to be eaten raw. If the pack is damaged or you have bought it loose from the butcher, remove the packaging and transfer the meat to a covered dish and store in the refrigerator. Ideally, fresh beef mince should be cooked and eaten on the day of purchase.

Minced beef will always contain some fat. This is why it is easy to brown in a non-stick pan without adding any oil – a technique that is the perfect start for many recipes. For some recipes, it is very important to drain off as much fat as possible after browning the meat – with or without additional oil – as the mixture needs to be quite dry. In fact, it is always worth checking the pan after browning minced beef and, if it does look a bit greasy, draining off the excess.

Equipment

All the recipes in this book can be prepared and cooked with the tools and equipment found in most kitchens – scales, chopping boards, knives, saucepans and frying pans, mixing bowls and so on. The only specialist pan suggested in one or two recipes is a wok – a large pan with sloping sides designed for stir-frying – but you can use a frying pan instead, although it is not quite so easy to keep the ingredients moving while they cook.

It is worth buying the best-quality pans you can afford because, if you look after them well, they will last many years. A pan with a thick, solid base, preferably ground rather than stamped flat, distributes heat well so that the food cooks evenly. Make sure that the handles are secure and lids fit tightly. Always use the correct-sized pan as one that is too small may cause ingredients to cook unevenly or boil over, while

one that is too large may result in the dish drying out. A flameproof casserole is extremely useful and can double as a large saucepan.

It is also worth buying good-quality knives and an efficient sharpener. Keep knives sharp, as not only are they more efficient when sharp, but they are also much safer. Blunt knives can easily slip and cut your hand. Store them in a knife block or a wall-mounted magnetic rack out of the reach of children. Do not store them in a drawer where other tools may damage the cutting edges. Always use a wooden or polyethylene chopping board when slicing or dicing, as hard materials, such as glass, metal or granite, can damage the blades.

About the Basic Mince Mix

As beef mince is so versatile, the basic mince mix is very flexible and easily adapted. Onions always feature, but in some recipes a different member of the onion family, such as shallots or spring onions, is substituted. Garlic is a valuable addition in many dishes, but it is optional as some people find its flavour too pungent.

Herbs, spices and flavourings are added to the basic mix to give each dish its unique character and quantities vary from a pinch to several tablespoons, depending on the strength of flavour. A huge range features throughout the book – fresh and dried herbs, hot and aromatic spices, sauces and condiments, fresh and dried chillies, to name just a few. Other additional ingredients, such as stock, canned or fresh tomatoes, potatoes, breadcrumbs and mushrooms, vary according to the type of dish.

Basic Mince Mix

Serves 4–6

* 1 kg/2 lb 4 oz fresh beef mince
* 1 onion, finely chopped (recipes may substitute Spanish onions, red onions, shallots or spring onions)
* 1 garlic clove, finely chopped (optional)
* salt and pepper

This is the basic mix that all 50 variations of minced beef dishes in the book are based on.

For each recipe the basic mix is highlighted (*) for easy reference, so then all you have to do is follow the easy steps each time and a world of delicious and tempting meals will await you.

Please note that the ingredient quantities vary from time to time so please check these carefully.

Easy

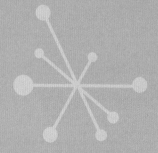

Beef & Tomato Soup

1. Heat the oil in a large saucepan. Add the onion and garlic and cook over a low heat, stirring occasionally, for 5 minutes, until softened. Stir in the chillies and tomatoes and cook for a further 5 minutes. Add the beef, increase the heat to medium and cook, breaking it up with a wooden spoon, for 6–8 minutes, until lightly browned.

2. Stir in the carrots, potatoes and parsley, pour in the stock and season to taste with salt and pepper. Bring to the boil, then reduce the heat, cover and simmer for 30 minutes, until the meat and vegetables are tender.

3. Taste and adjust the seasoning, adding salt and pepper if needed. Ladle the soup into warmed bowls, garnish with parsley and serve immediately with crusty rolls.

Serves 6

3 tbsp sunflower oil

1 onion, finely chopped

1 garlic clove, finely chopped

2 fresh red chillies, deseeded and finely chopped

4 large tomatoes, peeled and chopped

500 g/1 lb 2 oz fresh beef mince

2 carrots, diced

2 potatoes, diced

1–2 tbsp chopped fresh flat-leaf parsley, plus extra to garnish

1.2 litres/2 pints beef stock

salt and pepper

crusty rolls, to serve

Home-made Burgers

1. Put the beef, onion, parsley and Worcestershire sauce into a bowl, season to taste with salt and pepper and mix well with your hands until thoroughly combined.

2. Divide the mixture into six equal portions and shape into balls, then gently flatten into patties. If you have time, chill in the refrigerator for 30 minutes to firm up.

3. Heat the oil in a large frying pan. Add the burgers, in batches, and cook over a medium heat for 5–8 minutes on each side, turning them carefully with a fish slice. Remove from the pan and keep warm while you cook the remaining burgers.

4. Serve in toasted buns with lettuce leaves, tomato slices, gherkins and tomato ketchup.

Serves 6

* 1 kg/2 lb 4 oz fresh beef mince
* 1 small onion, grated
1 tbsp chopped fresh parsley
2 tsp Worcestershire sauce
2 tbsp sunflower oil
* salt and pepper

To serve
6 burger buns, split and toasted
lettuce leaves
tomato slices
gherkins, sliced
tomato ketchup

Beef Keftas

1. Put the beef, onion, garlic, coriander and spices into a bowl and season to taste with salt and pepper. Add the egg and mix well with your hands until thoroughly combined and very smooth. Cover the bowl with clingfilm and chill in the refrigerator for 30 minutes.

2. Meanwhile, mix together the chopped mint and the yogurt in a bowl and season to taste with salt. Cover with clingfilm and chill until required.

3. Preheat the grill or barbecue. Remove the beef mixture from the refrigerator, scoop up pieces with your hands and shape into small ovals about 2 cm/¾ inch thick. Thread the keftas onto metal or pre-soaked wooden skewers, with three to each skewer.

4. Brush the grill rack or barbecue grill with oil. Cook the skewers, in batches if necessary, under the preheated grill or over hot coals, turning occasionally, for 10–12 minutes, until cooked through. Garnish with mint leaves and lime wedges and serve immediately with the minted yogurt.

Serves 6–8

* 1 kg/2 lb 4 oz fresh beef mince
* 1 Spanish onion, grated
* 3 garlic cloves, very finely chopped
4 tbsp chopped fresh coriander
1 tsp ground cumin
½ tsp ground cinnamon
½ tsp ground turmeric
1 tsp paprika
1 large egg, lightly beaten
3 tbsp finely chopped fresh mint, plus extra leaves to garnish
150 ml/5 fl oz natural yogurt
sunflower oil, for brushing
* salt and pepper
lime wedges, to garnish

4

Beef & Noodles

1. Cook the noodles according to the packet instructions, then drain and refresh under cold running water. Tip them into a bowl, add 1 tablespoon of the sesame oil and toss to coat.

2. Heat a wok over a medium heat, then add the groundnut oil, swirl it around the wok and heat. Add the onion and stir-fry for a few minutes, until softened. Add the beef and stir-fry, breaking it up with a wooden spoon, for 3–5 minutes, until evenly browned.

3. Stir in the ginger, chilli and five-spice powder and cook, stirring constantly, for 1 minute, then add the carrots, red pepper and mangetout. Stir-fry for a further 4 minutes.

4. Add the beansprouts, the remaining sesame oil and the noodles and stir-fry for a further 2 minutes. Serve immediately.

Serves 6

450 g/1 lb dried egg noodles

2 tbsp sesame oil

2 tbsp groundnut oil

1 onion, finely chopped

650 g/1 lb 7 oz fresh beef mince

2.5-cm/1-inch piece fresh ginger, thinly sliced

1 fresh red chilli, deseeded and thinly sliced

1½ tsp Chinese five-spice powder

2 carrots, thinly sliced diagonally

1 red pepper, deseeded and diced

85 g/3 oz mangetout

175 g/6 oz fresh beansprouts

Quick Curry

1. Heat half the oil in a large saucepan. Add the onion, green pepper, cumin seeds, cardamom pods and bay leaves and cook over a low heat, stirring constantly, for 2–3 minutes, until the spices give off their aroma. Add the tomatoes and cook, stirring frequently, for 10 minutes.

2. Meanwhile, heat the remaining oil in a frying pan. Add the garlic and cook, stirring frequently, for 1 minute, then add the beef, ground coriander, turmeric and chilli powder. Cook over a medium heat, stirring constantly and breaking up the meat with a wooden spoon, for 4–5 minutes, until the meat is evenly browned. Transfer the mixture to the saucepan.

3. Pour in the stock and bring to the boil, then reduce the heat, cover and simmer, stirring occasionally, for 20–25 minutes. If the mixture seems to be drying out, add a little water.

4. Remove and discard the bay leaves and cardamom pods, then season to taste with salt. Scatter over the chopped coriander and serve immediately with rice and naan bread.

Serves 4

4 tbsp groundnut oil

1 large onion, finely chopped

1 green pepper, deseeded and diced

1 tsp cumin seeds

4 green cardamom pods

2 bay leaves

500 g/1 lb 2 oz tomatoes, peeled and chopped

2 garlic cloves, finely chopped

450 g/1 lb fresh beef mince

2 tsp ground coriander

2 tsp ground turmeric

1 tsp chilli powder

600 ml/1 pint beef stock

2 tbsp chopped fresh coriander

salt

cooked rice and naan bread, to serve

Tex-Mex Pizza

1. Preheat the oven to 200°C/400°F/Gas Mark 6. Brush a baking sheet with oil. Heat the oil in a saucepan. Add the onion and garlic and cook over a low heat, stirring occasionally, for 5 minutes, until softened. Add the beef, increase the heat to medium and cook, stirring frequently and breaking it up with a wooden spoon, for 5–8 minutes, until evenly browned.

2. Drain off any excess fat. Stir in the cumin, jalapeño chillies and refried beans, pour in the water and season to taste with salt. Reduce the heat and simmer gently for 5 minutes, then remove from the heat.

3. Meanwhile, make the pizza dough. Sift the flour and salt into a bowl. Add the butter and rub it in with your fingertips until the mixture resembles breadcrumbs. Pour in 100 ml/3½ fl oz of the milk and mix with a round-bladed knife to a soft dough, adding the remaining milk if necessary. Turn out the dough onto a lightly floured surface and knead gently. Roll out to a 25-cm/10-inch round and transfer to the prepared baking sheet. Push up the edge slightly all around to make a rim.

4. Spread the beef mixture evenly over the pizza base and sprinkle with the cheese. Bake in the preheated oven for 18–20 minutes, until the cheese has melted and is golden. Top with avocado slices, red chilli slices and soured cream and serve immediately.

Serves 2

2 tbsp sunflower oil, plus extra for brushing

1 small onion, finely chopped

1 garlic clove, finely chopped

225 g/8 oz fresh beef mince

1 tsp ground cumin

4 pickled jalapeño chillies, drained and finely chopped

400 g/14 oz canned refried beans

150 ml/5 fl oz water

250 g/9 oz Cheddar cheese, grated

salt

Pizza dough
175 g/6 oz self-raising flour, plus extra for dusting

pinch of salt

25 g/1 oz butter, cut into small pieces

100–125 ml/3½–4 fl oz milk

To serve
avocado slices

fresh red chilli slices

soured cream

One-pot Pasta

1. Heat the oil in a large saucepan with a tight-fitting lid. Add the onion, garlic, celery and carrot and cook over a low heat, stirring occasionally, for 5 minutes, until softened. Add the beef, increase the heat to medium and cook, stirring frequently and breaking it up with a wooden spoon, for 5–8 minutes, until evenly browned.

2. Add the mushrooms and cook for a further 3–4 minutes. Add the tomatoes, tomato purée, sugar, herbs, pasta and wine. Stir in the concentrated stock, add just enough water to cover and stir well.

3. Reduce the heat, cover tightly and simmer gently for 15–20 minutes, until the pasta is tender but still firm to the bite and the sauce has thickened. Season to taste with salt and pepper and serve immediately.

Serves 4

2 tbsp olive oil

1 onion, chopped

1 garlic clove, finely chopped

1 celery stick, chopped

1 carrot, chopped

500 g/1 lb 2 oz fresh beef mince

115 g/4 oz mushrooms, sliced

400 g/14 oz canned chopped tomatoes

1 tbsp tomato purée

1 tsp sugar

pinch of dried oregano

1 tbsp chopped fresh flat-leaf parsley

175 g/6 oz dried fusilli

175 ml/6 fl oz red wine

1½ tbsp concentrated beef stock or 1 beef stock cube

salt and pepper

Cheat's Lasagne

1. Heat the oil in a saucepan. Add the beef, onion, garlic and carrot and cook over a medium heat, stirring frequently and breaking up the meat with a wooden spoon, for 5–8 minutes, until the beef is evenly browned.

2. Stir in the herbs, season to taste with salt and pepper and pour in the passata. Bring to the boil, then reduce the heat, cover and simmer for 15 minutes.

3. Meanwhile, preheat the oven to 190°C/375°F/Gas Mark 5. Mix the ricotta with the egg, stirring until smooth and thoroughly combined.

4. Make alternating layers of the beef mixture, lasagne sheets, ricotta mixture and mozzarella in an ovenproof dish, ending with a layer of mozzarella. Bake in the preheated oven for 40–45 minutes, until the topping is golden and bubbling. Leave to stand for 5 minutes before serving.

Serves 6

2 tbsp olive oil

500 g/1 lb 2 oz fresh beef mince

1 onion, chopped

1 garlic clove, finely chopped

1 carrot, diced

1 tbsp chopped fresh flat-leaf parsley

6 fresh basil leaves, torn

600 ml/1 pint passata

550 g/1 lb 4 oz ricotta cheese

1 egg, lightly beaten

8 no pre-cook lasagne sheets

225 g/8 oz mozzarella cheese, grated

salt and pepper

Beefy Baked Potatoes

① Preheat the oven to 220°C/425°F/Gas Mark 7. Prick the potatoes all over with a fork. Put them directly on an oven shelf and bake in the preheated oven for 1¼–1½ hours, until soft.

② Meanwhile, heat the oil in a saucepan. Add the chopped spring onions and the garlic and cook over a low heat, stirring occasionally for 5 minutes, until softened. Add the beef, increase the heat to medium and cook, stirring frequently and breaking it up with a wooden spoon, for 8–10 minutes, until evenly browned.

③ Stir in the tomato purée, soy sauce and 150 ml/5 fl oz of the stock and season to taste with salt and pepper. Reduce the heat, cover and simmer, stirring occasionally, for 25–30 minutes, adding more stock if the mixture seems to be drying out.

④ Remove the potatoes from the oven and put them on four individual plates. Cut a cross in the centre of each and squeeze gently, then ladle the beef mixture over them. Garnish with shredded spring onions and serve immediately.

Serves 4

4 large baking potatoes

2 tbsp sunflower oil

2 spring onions, finely chopped, plus extra shredded spring onions to garnish

1 garlic clove, finely chopped

350 g/12 oz fresh beef mince

1 tbsp tomato purée

1 tbsp light soy sauce

150–200 ml/5–7 fl oz beef stock

salt and pepper

Rissoles

1. Cook the potatoes in a large saucepan of salted boiling water for 25–30 minutes, until tender but not falling apart. Drain well, tip into a bowl and mash until smooth.

2. Add the onion, beef, chives, parsley and Worcestershire sauce and season to taste with salt and pepper. Mix well until thoroughly combined. If you have time, cover the bowl with clingfilm and chill the mixture in the refrigerator for 30–45 minutes to firm up.

3. Dampen your hands and shape the mixture into 12 sausage-shaped rissoles. Lightly beat the eggs in a shallow dish, spread out the flour in a second shallow dish and spread out the breadcrumbs in a third shallow dish.

4. Pour oil into a large frying pan to a depth of about 1 cm/ ½ inch and heat. Meanwhile, coat the rissoles first in the flour, then in the beaten egg and, finally, in the breadcrumbs. Shake off any excess.

5. Add the rissoles to the frying pan, in batches if necessary, and cook over a medium heat, turning occasionally, for 8–10 minutes, until crisp, evenly browned and cooked through. Remove from the pan with a fish slice and keep warm while you cook the remaining rissoles. Serve immediately.

Serves 6

1 kg/2 lb 4 oz potatoes

1 onion, finely chopped

500 g/1 lb 2 oz fresh beef mince

1 tbsp snipped fresh chives

1 tbsp chopped fresh parsley

2 tsp Worcestershire sauce or tomato ketchup

3 eggs

3 tbsp plain flour

175 g/6 oz fresh breadcrumbs

sunflower oil, for shallow-frying

salt and pepper

Favourite

11

Swedish Meatballs

1. Cook the potatoes in a saucepan of salted boiling water for 20–25 minutes, until tender but not falling apart. Drain, tip into a bowl, mash well and leave to cool slightly.

2. Add the fresh breadcrumbs, beef, onion, egg, sugar and spices to the bowl. Season to taste with salt and pepper and mix well until thoroughly combined. Shape the mixture into walnut-sized balls, rolling them between the palms of your hands. Roll the meatballs in the dry breadcrumbs until thoroughly coated.

3. Melt the butter in a large frying pan. Add the meatballs, in batches, and cook over a medium heat, stirring and turning occasionally, for 10 minutes, until golden brown all over and cooked through. Remove with a slotted spoon, drain on kitchen paper and keep warm while you cook the remaining meatballs.

4. When all the meatballs have been cooked, keep them warm while you make the sauce. Stir the flour into the frying pan and cook, stirring constantly, for 1 minute. Remove the pan from the heat and gradually stir in the stock, then add the cream. Season to taste with salt and pepper, return the pan to a low heat and cook, stirring constantly, until thickened and smooth.

5. Return the meatballs to the pan and simmer for 10 minutes. Serve immediately.

Serves 4

2 potatoes, cut into chunks

25 g/1 oz fresh breadcrumbs

650 g/1 lb 7 oz fresh beef mince

1 small onion, grated

1 egg, lightly beaten

1 tsp brown sugar

pinch of each grated nutmeg, ground allspice, ground ginger and ground cloves

55 g/2 oz fine dry breadcrumbs

85 g/3 oz butter

salt and pepper

Sauce
2 tbsp plain flour

225 ml/8 fl oz beef stock

225 ml/8 fl oz double cream

salt and pepper

Meatloaf

1. Preheat the oven to 160°C/325°F/Gas Mark 3. Put all of the ingredients, except for the bacon rashers, into a bowl. Season to taste with pepper and mix well until thoroughly combined.

2. Spoon the mixture into a 900-g/2-lb loaf tin, pressing it down well. Cover with the bacon.

3. Put the loaf tin into a roasting tin and pour in boiling water to come about halfway up the sides. Bake in the preheated oven for 1½ hours, until a wooden cocktail stick inserted into the centre comes out clean.

4. For the tomato sauce, heat the oil in a saucepan. Add the onion and garlic and cook over a low heat, stirring occasionally, for 5 minutes, until softened. Mix the tomato purée with the water in a small bowl. Add to the saucepan with the tomatoes and bring to the boil, then simmer, stirring occasionally, for 15–20 minutes, until thickened. Transfer the sauce to a food processor or blender and process to a purée. Pour into a clean pan and stir in the sugar to taste. Cover and leave to cool.

5. Remove the tin from the oven and pour off any fat. Leave to cool for 1 hour. Run a round-bladed knife around the sides of the tin and turn out onto a plate. Wrap the meatloaf in foil and chill in the refrigerator for 4 hours, or overnight. Cut into slices and serve with the tomato sauce.

Serves 4

- 500 g/1 lb 2 oz fresh beef mince
- 1 onion, finely chopped
- 2 garlic cloves, finely chopped (optional)
- 115 g/4 oz mushrooms, finely chopped
- 85 g/3 oz fresh breadcrumbs
- 2 eggs, lightly beaten
- 2 tsp Dijon mustard
- 1 tsp Worcestershire sauce
- 1 tsp celery salt
- 1 tbsp chopped fresh parsley
- 8–10 streaky bacon rashers
- pepper

Tomato sauce
- 2 tbsp sunflower oil
- 1 onion, finely chopped
- 2 garlic cloves, finely chopped
- 2 tbsp tomato purée
- 100 ml/3½ fl oz water
- 400 g/14 oz canned chopped tomatoes
- 1–2 tsp brown sugar

Spaghetti Bolognese

1. Heat the oil in a saucepan. Add the pancetta, onion, carrot, celery and garlic and cook over a low heat, stirring occasionally, for 5 minutes, until softened.

2. Add the beef, increase the heat to medium and cook, stirring frequently and breaking up the meat with a wooden spoon, for 8–10 minutes, until evenly browned. Stir in the mushrooms and chicken livers, if using, and cook, stirring frequently, for a further 3–4 minutes.

3. Stir in the tomatoes, tomato purée, wine, stock, bay leaf and oregano. Season to taste with salt and pepper, then bring to the boil. Reduce the heat, cover and simmer, stirring occasionally, for 1 hour.

4. When the sauce is nearly ready, bring a saucepan of salted water to the boil. Add the spaghetti, return to the boil and cook for 8–10 minutes, until tender but still firm to the bite. Drain the pasta, return it to the pan and toss with the butter.

5. Remove the sauce from the heat and discard the bay leaf. Add the spaghetti and toss well, then transfer to a warmed serving dish. Sprinkle with Parmesan cheese shavings and serve immediately.

Serves 4

2 tbsp olive oil

85 g/3 oz pancetta or bacon, diced

1 onion, finely chopped

1 carrot, finely chopped

1 celery stick, finely chopped

2 garlic cloves, finely chopped

500 g/1 lb 2 oz fresh beef mince

115 g/4 oz mushrooms, thinly sliced

115 g/4 oz chicken livers, finely chopped (optional)

400 g/14 oz canned chopped tomatoes

2 tbsp tomato purée

150 ml/5 fl oz white wine

300 ml/10 fl oz beef stock

1 bay leaf

pinch of dried oregano

450 g/1 lb dried spaghetti

25 g/1 oz butter

salt and pepper

Parmesan cheese shavings, to serve

Meaty Macaroni Cheese

1. Heat the oil in a saucepan. Add the onion and garlic and cook over a low heat, stirring occasionally, for 5 minutes, until softened. Add the beef, increase the heat to medium and cook, breaking it up with a wooden spoon, for 8–10 minutes, until lightly browned all over. Stir in the sweetcorn, tomatoes and mixed herbs and season to taste with salt and pepper. Reduce the heat, cover and simmer, stirring occasionally, for 25–30 minutes.

2. Bring a large saucepan of salted water to the boil. Add the macaroni, return to the boil and cook for 10 minutes, until tender but still firm to the bite.

3. Meanwhile, preheat the grill. Melt the butter in a separate saucepan. Sprinkle in the flour and cook, stirring constantly, for 2 minutes. Remove the pan from the heat and gradually stir in the milk, a little at a time. Return the pan to the heat and bring to the boil, stirring constantly. Reduce the heat and simmer the sauce, stirring constantly, for 5 minutes, until thickened and smooth. Remove the pan from the heat and stir in the mustard and 150 g/5½ oz of the cheese. Stir well until the cheese has melted.

4. Drain the macaroni and tip it into the cheese sauce, stirring well to mix. Spoon the beef mixture into a baking dish, then cover with the macaroni mixture. Sprinkle with the remaining cheese and cook under the preheated grill for 4–5 minutes, until the top is golden and bubbling. Serve immediately.

Serves 6

2 tbsp olive oil

1 onion, chopped

1 garlic clove, finely chopped

500 g/1 lb 2 oz fresh beef mince

200 g/7 oz canned sweetcorn, drained

400 g/14 oz canned chopped tomatoes

1 tsp dried mixed herbs

225 g/8 oz dried macaroni

40 g/1½ oz butter

40 g/1½ oz plain flour

500 ml/18 fl oz milk

2 tsp Dijon mustard

200 g/7 oz Cheddar cheese, grated

salt and pepper

Spaghetti & Meatballs

1. Heat the oil in a frying pan. Add the chopped onion and garlic and cook over a low heat, for 5 minutes, until softened. Remove from the heat and tip the mixture into a bowl with the thyme, beef, breadcrumbs and egg. Season to taste with salt and pepper and mix well. Shape into 20 meatballs.

2. Heat a large non-stick frying pan over a low–medium heat. Add the meatballs and cook, stirring gently and turning frequently, for 15 minutes, until lightly browned all over.

   Meanwhile, preheat the grill. Put the onion wedges and pepper halves, skin-side up, on a grill rack and cook under the preheated grill, turning frequently, for 10 minutes, until the pepper skins are blistered and charred. Put the peppers into a plastic bag, tie the top and leave to cool. Set the onion wedges aside.

3. Peel off the pepper skins. Roughly chop the flesh and put it into a food processor or blender with the onion wedges and tomatoes. Process to a smooth purée and season to taste with salt and pepper. Pour into a saucepan with the bay leaf and bring to the boil. Reduce the heat and simmer, stirring occasionally, for 10 minutes. Remove and discard the bay leaf.

4. Meanwhile, bring a saucepan of salted water to the boil. Add the spaghetti, return to the boil and cook for 8–10 minutes, until tender but still firm to the bite. Drain the spaghetti and serve immediately with the meatballs and sauce.

Serves 4

1 tbsp olive oil

1 small onion, finely chopped

2 garlic cloves, finely chopped

2 fresh thyme sprigs, finely chopped

650 g/1 lb 7 oz fresh beef mince

25 g/1 oz fresh breadcrumbs

1 egg, lightly beaten

450 g/1 lb dried spaghetti

salt and pepper

Sauce

1 onion, cut into wedges

3 red peppers, halved and deseeded

400 g/14 oz canned chopped tomatoes

1 bay leaf

salt and pepper

Classic Lasagne

1. Heat the oil in a saucepan. Add the bacon and cook, stirring frequently, for 3–4 minutes. Add the onion, garlic, carrots and celery and cook over a low heat, stirring occasionally, for 5 minutes, until softened. Add the beef, increase the heat to medium and cook, stirring frequently and breaking it up with a wooden spoon, for 8–10 minutes, until evenly browned. Stir in the oregano, parsley and tomatoes. Season to taste with salt and pepper, then reduce the heat and simmer, stirring occasionally, for 30 minutes.

2. Preheat the oven to 200°C/400°F/Gas Mark 6. Meanwhile, make the Béchamel sauce. Pour the milk into a saucepan and add the peppercorns, onion, bay leaf and mace. Bring to the boil, then remove from the heat and leave to infuse for 10 minutes. Strain the milk into a jug and discard the flavourings. Melt the butter in a separate saucepan. Stir in the flour and cook, stirring constantly, for 2 minutes. Gradually stir in the flavoured milk, a little at a time, and bring to the boil, stirring constantly. Reduce the heat and simmer, stirring constantly for a few minutes, until thickened and smooth. Remove from the heat and season to taste with salt and pepper.

3. Make alternating layers of the beef mixture, lasagne sheets, Béchamel sauce and Parmesan in an ovenproof dish, ending with a layer of Béchamel sauce sprinkled with Parmesan. Bake in the preheated oven for 30 minutes, until golden brown. Leave to stand for 10 minutes before serving.

Serves 6

3 tbsp olive oil

2 bacon rashers, chopped

1 Spanish onion, chopped

2 garlic cloves, finely chopped

2 carrots, chopped

2 celery sticks, chopped

350 g/12 oz fresh beef mince

pinch of dried oregano

1 tbsp chopped fresh parsley

400 g/14 oz canned chopped tomatoes

225 g/8 oz no pre-cook lasagne sheets

115 g/4 oz Parmesan cheese, grated

salt and pepper

Béchamel sauce

500 ml/18 fl oz milk

6 black peppercorns

1 slice onion

1 bay leaf

1 mace blade

55 g/2 oz butter

55 g/2 oz plain flour

salt and pepper

Sloppy Joes

1. Put the beef, onion, garlic and green pepper into a non-stick frying pan and cook over a medium heat, stirring frequently and breaking up the beef with a wooden spoon, for 8–10 minutes, until the beef is evenly browned. Carefully drain off the fat.

2. Stir in the mustard, tomato ketchup, vinegar, brown sugar and chilli powder, if using. Season to taste with salt and pepper. Reduce the heat and simmer, stirring occasionally, for 30 minutes.

3. Divide the mixture among the burger buns and serve immediately.

Serves 4

- 450 g/1 lb fresh beef mince
- 1 onion, chopped
- 1 garlic clove, chopped
- 1 green pepper, deseeded and chopped
- 1 tbsp American mustard
- 175 ml/6 fl oz tomato ketchup
- 1 tsp white vinegar
- 1 tbsp brown sugar
- pinch of chilli powder, ground cloves or paprika (optional)
- 4 burger buns, split
- salt and pepper

Cheese-stuffed Burgers

1. Preheat the grill. Put the beef, onion, garlic, horseradish and thyme into a bowl. Season to taste with salt and pepper and mix well until thoroughly combined. Divide the mixture into eight portions and shape each portion into a patty shape.

2. Sprinkle the cheese over four of the patties and top with the remaining patties. Gently press the edges together, smoothing them with a palette knife to enclose the cheese completely.

3. Cook under the preheated grill for 5–6 minutes on each side, turning them carefully with a fish slice. Serve in the toasted buns with rocket leaves.

Serves 4

- 500 g/1 lb 2 oz fresh beef mince
- 1 onion, finely chopped
- 1 garlic clove, finely chopped
- 1 tsp creamed horseradish
- 1 tbsp chopped fresh thyme
- 55 g/2 oz Gorgonzola, Lancashire or feta cheese, crumbled
- 4 burger buns, split and toasted
- salt and pepper
- rocket leaves, to serve

19

Beef in Pitta Pockets

1. Heat the oil in a frying pan. Add the onion and garlic and cook over a low heat, stirring occasionally, for 5 minutes, until softened. Add the beef, increase the heat to medium and cook, stirring frequently and breaking it up with a wooden spoon, for 8–10 minutes, until evenly browned. Stir in the tomatoes, cumin, ground coriander and turmeric. Season to taste with salt and pepper, reduce the heat and simmer, stirring occasionally, for 15–20 minutes.

2. Meanwhile, dry-fry the pine kernels in a small frying pan, stirring constantly, until golden. Stir the pine kernels and chopped coriander into the meat mixture and simmer for 3–4 minutes.

3. To serve, cut a slit in the side of each pitta bread to make a pocket. Put a little of the beef mixture into each pocket with some chopped cucumber and shredded lettuce. Top with a spoonful of soured cream and serve immediately.

Serves 4

2 tbsp olive oil

1 onion, chopped

1 garlic clove, chopped

500 g/1 lb 2 oz fresh beef mince

200 g/7 oz canned chopped tomatoes

1 tsp ground cumin

1 tsp ground coriander

½ tsp ground turmeric

85 g/3 oz pine kernels

2 tbsp chopped fresh coriander

salt and pepper

To serve
8 pitta breads, warmed

chopped cucumber

shredded lettuce

soured cream

20

Salisbury Steak

1. Put the onion, breadcrumbs and egg into a bowl and mix well. Mix together the undiluted soup, horseradish, Worcestershire sauce and mustard in a separate bowl, stirring until thoroughly combined.

2. Add 4 tablespoons of the soup mixture to the onion mixture, then stir in the beef and season to taste with salt and pepper. Mix well until thoroughly combined. Divide the mixture into six portions and shape them into patties.

3. Heat the oil in a large frying pan. Add the patties and cook over a medium heat for 3–4 minutes on each side, until lightly browned.

4. Stir the stock into the remaining soup mixture and pour it into the pan. Reduce the heat, cover and simmer for 12–15 minutes, until the patties are cooked through. Garnish with parsley and serve immediately.

Serves 6

* 1 small onion, finely chopped

25 g/1 oz dry breadcrumbs

1 egg, lightly beaten

300 ml/10 fl oz canned condensed cream of mushroom soup

1 tsp creamed horseradish

1 tbsp Worcestershire sauce

1 tbsp Dijon mustard

* 700 g/1 lb 9 oz fresh beef mince

2 tbsp sunflower oil

125 ml/4 fl oz beef stock

* salt and pepper

chopped fresh parsley, to garnish

Comforting

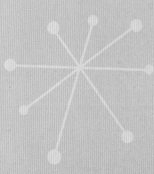

21

Tamale Pie

1. Preheat the oven to 190°C/375°F/Gas Mark 5. Heat the oil in a large frying pan. Add the onion and cook over a low heat, stirring occasionally, for 5 minutes, until softened.

2. Add the beef, increase the heat to medium and cook, stirring frequently and breaking it up with a wooden spoon, for 8–10 minutes, until evenly browned. Stir in the chilli powder, tomatoes, sweetcorn, olives and soured cream and season to taste with salt, then transfer the mixture to an ovenproof dish.

3. Put the cornmeal, baking powder, butter and milk in a food processor or blender and process until combined. With the motor running, gradually add enough of the hot stock through the feeder tube to make a thick, smooth mixture.

4. Pour the cornmeal mixture over the beef mixture and smooth the surface with a palette knife. Bake in the preheated oven for 20 minutes, until the topping is just beginning to brown. Remove from the oven, sprinkle with the cheese, then return to the oven and bake for a further 15 minutes, until golden and bubbling.

Serves 6

2 tbsp corn oil

1 onion, finely chopped

350 g/12 oz fresh beef mince

1½ tsp chilli powder

200 g/7 oz canned chopped tomatoes

140 g/5 oz canned sweetcorn, drained

2 tbsp chopped stoned black olives

100 ml/3½ fl oz soured cream

125 g/4½ oz cornmeal or coarse polenta

½ tsp baking powder

55 g/2 oz butter, cut into pieces

3 tbsp milk

about 225 ml/8 fl oz hot chicken stock

85 g/3 oz Cheddar cheese, grated

salt

22

Cottage Pie

1. Cook the potatoes in a large saucepan of salted boiling water for 20–25 minutes, until tender but not falling apart.

2. Meanwhile, heat the oil in a saucepan. Add the onion, garlic (if using) and carrots and cook over a low heat, stirring occasionally, for 5 minutes, until the onion has softened. Increase the heat to medium, add the beef and cook, stirring frequently and breaking it up with a wooden spoon, for 8–10 minutes, until evenly browned.

3. Add the mushrooms and cook for 2 minutes, then pour in the stock and stir in the sugar and Worcestershire sauce. Season to taste with salt and pepper. Reduce the heat, cover and simmer for 20 minutes.

4. Preheat the oven to 200°C/400°F/Gas Mark 6. Drain the potatoes, return to the pan and mash well, then stir in three quarters of the cheese.

5. Spoon the meat mixture into an ovenproof dish and spread the mashed potato over the top to cover. Sprinkle with the remaining cheese and bake in the preheated oven for 20 minutes, until the topping is golden brown. Serve immediately.

Serves 6

650 g/1 lb 7 oz potatoes, cut into chunks

2 tbsp sunflower oil

1 onion, chopped

1 garlic clove, chopped (optional)

2 carrots, chopped

500 g/1 lb 2 oz fresh beef mince

115 g/4 oz mushrooms, sliced

300 ml/10 fl oz hot beef stock

1 tsp sugar

1 tbsp Worcestershire sauce

115 g/4 oz Cheddar cheese, grated

salt and pepper

23

Beef with Garlic Potatoes

1. Preheat the oven to 180°C/350°F/Gas Mark 4. Parboil the potatoes in a saucepan of salted boiling water for 15 minutes, then drain and leave to cool.

2. Meanwhile, heat 1 tablespoon of the oil in a large saucepan. Add the onion and cook over a low heat, stirring occasionally, for 5 minutes, until softened.

3. Add the beef, increase the heat to medium and cook, stirring frequently and breaking it up with a wooden spoon, for 8–10 minutes, until evenly browned. Add the carrots and tomatoes. Stir the cornflour into the stock, then stir the mixture into the pan. Season to taste with salt and pepper. Stir in the parsley and sage and bring to the boil, then reduce the heat and simmer for 5 minutes.

4. Meanwhile, cut the potatoes into slices. Mix together the garlic and the remaining oil in a small bowl and season to taste with salt and pepper.

5. Transfer the beef mixture to an ovenproof dish and arrange the potato slices on top. Brush the garlic-flavoured oil over them and bake in the preheated oven for 30–35 minutes, until the topping is golden brown. Serve immediately.

Serves 4

500 g/1 lb 2 oz potatoes

3 tbsp olive oil

* 1 onion, chopped

* 500 g/1 lb 2 oz fresh beef mince

225 g/8 oz carrots, chopped

4 tomatoes, peeled and chopped

1 tsp cornflour

300 ml/10 fl oz hot beef stock

1 tbsp chopped fresh parsley

1 tsp chopped fresh sage

* 3 garlic cloves, very finely chopped

* salt and pepper

24

Braised Beef Burgers

1. Put the beef, garlic, shallot, celery, breadcrumbs, basil and egg into a bowl and season to taste with salt and pepper. Mix well until thoroughly combined, then divide the mixture into four equal portions and shape them into patties.

2. Heat the oil in a frying pan. Add the burgers and cook over a medium heat for 3 minutes on each side, until browned. Remove from the pan and keep warm.

3. Add the onion to the pan and cook over a low heat, stirring occasionally, for 5 minutes, until softened. Drain off as much fat as possible. Return the pan to the heat and stir in the stock, then add the bay leaf and season to taste with salt. Return the burgers to the pan and simmer gently for 25 minutes.

4. Transfer the burgers to warmed individual plates. Remove and discard the bay leaf, then pour the sauce over the burgers and serve immediately.

Serves 4

* 650 g/1 lb 7 oz fresh beef mince
* 2 garlic cloves, finely chopped
* 1 shallot, finely chopped
  1 celery stick, finely chopped
  25 g/1 oz fresh breadcrumbs
  1 fresh basil sprig, finely chopped
  1 egg, lightly beaten
  2 tbsp sunflower oil
  1 small onion, chopped
  225 ml/8 fl oz beef stock
  1 bay leaf
* salt and pepper

Layered Beef & Feta

1. Heat half the oil in a large frying pan. Add the onion and garlic and cook over a low heat, stirring occasionally, for 5 minutes, until softened. Add the beef, increase the heat to medium and cook, stirring frequently and breaking up the meat with a wooden spoon, for 8–10 minutes, until evenly browned. Drain off the fat and return the pan to the heat. Stir in the tomato purée and cook for a further 2–3 minutes, then stir in the tomatoes, Worcestershire sauce and oregano. Season to taste with salt and pepper. Reduce the heat, cover and simmer for 30 minutes.

2. Meanwhile, cook the potatoes in a saucepan of salted boiling water for 20–25 minutes, until tender but not falling apart. Drain and leave to cool slightly, then cut into thick slices.

3. Preheat the oven to 180°C/350°F/Gas Mark 4. Brush the aubergine slices with the remaining oil. Heat a large heavy-based frying pan. Add the aubergine slices, in batches, and cook over a medium heat for 3 minutes on each side, until softened. Drain on kitchen paper.

4. Transfer the beef mixture to an ovenproof dish and cover with the potato slices, followed by the aubergine slices. Crumble the feta over the top. Mix the yogurt, eggs and half the Parmesan in a bowl and pour evenly over the dish. Sprinkle with the remaining Parmesan and bake in the preheated oven for 30–35 minutes, until golden brown. Serve immediately.

Serves 6

- 4 tbsp olive oil
- 1 onion, chopped
- 2 garlic cloves, finely chopped
- 650 g/1 lb 7 oz fresh beef mince
- 1½ tbsp tomato purée
- 600 g/1 lb 5 oz canned chopped tomatoes
- 2 tbsp Worcestershire sauce
- 1 tbsp chopped fresh oregano
- 750 g/1 lb 10 oz potatoes
- 2 aubergines, sliced
- 150 g/5½ oz feta cheese
- 600 ml/1 pint Greek-style yogurt
- 3 large eggs, lightly beaten
- 40 g/1½ oz Parmesan cheese, grated
- salt and pepper

Beef & Cheese Cobbler

1. Preheat the oven to 180°C/350°F/Gas Mark 4. Heat the oil in a frying pan. Add the beef and cook over a medium heat, stirring frequently and breaking it up with a wooden spoon, for 8–10 minutes, until evenly browned.

2. Remove the pan from the heat and spoon the beef into a casserole, then stir in the plain flour. Add the onions, tomato ketchup, thyme and bay leaf and season to taste with salt and pepper. Pour in the stock and stir well, then cover and bake in the preheated oven for 1 hour.

3. Meanwhile, sift the self-raising flour, mustard powder and salt into a bowl. Add the butter and rub it in with your fingertips until the mixture resembles breadcrumbs. Stir in the cheese, Tabasco sauce and enough water to mix to a soft dough.

4. Roll out the dough to a thickness of 1 cm/½ inch on a lightly floured surface, then stamp out rounds with a 6-cm/2½-inch fluted round cutter.

5. Remove the casserole from the oven and take off the lid. Remove and discard the bay leaf. Cover the beef mixture with the dough rounds and brush them with milk. Return the casserole, without the lid, to the oven and bake for a further 35 minutes, until the topping is golden brown. Serve immediately.

Serves 4

2 tbsp sunflower oil

500 g/1 lb 2 oz fresh beef mince

2 tbsp plain flour

500 g/1 lb 2 oz onions, cut into wedges

2 tbsp tomato ketchup

1 tbsp chopped fresh thyme

1 bay leaf

300 ml/10 fl oz beef stock

salt and pepper

Cobbler topping

225 g/8 oz self-raising flour, plus extra for dusting

½ tsp mustard powder

pinch of salt

40 g/1½ oz butter, cut into small pieces

85 g/3 oz Cheddar cheese, grated

dash of Tabasco sauce

milk, for glazing

Greek Baked Pasta

1. Heat half the oil in a saucepan. Add the onion and garlic and cook over a low heat, stirring occasionally, for 5 minutes, until softened. Add the beef, increase the heat to medium and cook, stirring frequently and breaking it up with a wooden spoon, for 8–10 minutes, until evenly browned. Stir in the passata, sugar, vinegar and parsley and season to taste with salt and pepper. Reduce the heat, cover and simmer for 15 minutes, until thickened.

2. Meanwhile, preheat the oven to 180°C/350°F/Gas Mark 4. Preheat the grill. Brush a large ovenproof dish with oil. Bring a large saucepan of salted water to the boil. Add the macaroni, return to the boil and cook for 8–10 minutes, until tender but still firm to the bite. Drain and return to the pan. Stir in the remaining oil and the Gruyère.

3. Spread out the aubergine slices on a baking sheet and brush on both sides with oil. Cook under the preheated grill for 5 minutes on each side, until golden. Line the base and sides of the prepared dish with the aubergine slices.

4. Stir the eggs and Parmesan into the Béchamel sauce, then stir 3 tablespoons of the mixture into the beef mixture. Spoon half the macaroni evenly over the aubergine slices and pour in half the Béchamel mixture. Add the beef mixture and top with the remaining macaroni. Pour the remaining Béchamel mixture over the top. Bake in the preheated oven for 35–40 minutes, until golden brown. Leave to stand for 10 minutes before serving.

Serves 6

4 tbsp olive oil, plus extra for brushing

1 small onion, finely chopped

2 garlic cloves, finely chopped

500 g/1 lb 2 oz fresh beef mince

450 ml/16 fl oz passata

1 tsp sugar

2 tsp red wine vinegar

3 tbsp chopped fresh flat-leaf parsley

225 g/8 oz dried macaroni

225 g/8 oz Gruyère cheese, grated

1 kg/2 lb 4 oz aubergines, sliced lengthways

2 eggs, lightly beaten

100 g/3½ oz Parmesan cheese, grated

1 quantity Béchamel Sauce (see page 44)

salt and pepper

28

Bolognese Soufflé

1. Heat half the oil in a frying pan. Add the bacon and cook over a low heat, stirring occasionally, for 2–3 minutes. Add the onion and garlic and cook, stirring occasionally, for 5 minutes, until softened. Add the beef, increase the heat to medium and cook, stirring frequently and breaking it up with a wooden spoon, for 5–8 minutes, until evenly browned.

2. Stir in the tomatoes, tomato purée and thyme and season to taste with salt and pepper. Reduce the heat and simmer for 25 minutes, then remove from the heat and leave to cool.

3. Meanwhile, bring a saucepan of salted water to the boil. Add the pasta, return to the boil and cook for 8–10 minutes, until tender but still firm to the bite. Drain, return to the pan and toss with the remaining oil. Preheat the oven to 190°C/375°F/Gas Mark 5. Brush a soufflé dish with oil and sprinkle with the Parmesan.

4. Beat the egg yolks into the cooled beef mixture and fold in the pasta. Whisk the egg whites in a grease-free bowl until stiff, then fold into the beef and pasta mixture. Gently spoon into the prepared dish and bake in the preheated oven for 45 minutes, until risen and golden brown. Serve immediately.

Serves 4

- 2 tbsp olive oil, plus extra for brushing
- 4 bacon rashers, finely chopped
- 1 large onion, finely chopped
- 1 garlic clove, finely chopped
- 300 g/10½ oz fresh beef mince
- 400 g/14 oz canned chopped tomatoes
- 1 tbsp tomato purée
- 1 tbsp chopped fresh thyme
- 175 g/6 oz dried penne or other pasta shapes
- 25 g/1 oz Parmesan cheese, grated
- 3 eggs, separated
- salt and pepper

29

Beef & Vegetable Gratin

1. Heat the oil in a large saucepan. Add the garlic and onions and cook over a low heat, stirring occasionally, for 8–10 minutes, until golden brown. Add the beef, increase the heat to medium and cook, stirring frequently and breaking it up with a wooden spoon, for 8–10 minutes, until evenly browned. Stir in the courgettes, carrots, red pepper and raisins and season to taste with salt and pepper. Reduce the heat, cover and simmer for 25 minutes.

2. Meanwhile, preheat the oven to 180°C/350°F/Gas Mark 4. Melt the butter in a saucepan. Add the flour and cook over a low heat, stirring constantly, for 2 minutes. Remove the pan from the heat and gradually stir in the milk, a little at a time, until smooth. Return the pan to the heat and bring to the boil, stirring constantly, then cook, stirring, for a few minutes more, until thickened. Remove the pan from the heat and stir in the cheese until melted.

3. Stir the sweetcorn, beans and parsley into the beef mixture and simmer for a further 3 minutes, then remove the pan from the heat. Spoon the mixture into an ovenproof dish.

4. Lightly beat the egg yolks in a bowl with a fork, then stir in 4 tablespoons of the cheese sauce. Stir the egg yolk mixture into the cheese sauce and pour it over the meat mixture to cover. Bake in the preheated oven for 25–30 minutes, until the topping is golden brown. Serve immediately.

Serves 6–8

3 tbsp sunflower oil

2 garlic cloves, finely chopped

2 onions, sliced

1 kg/2 lb 4 oz fresh beef mince

500 g/1 lb 2 oz courgettes, thinly sliced

300 g/10½ oz carrots, thinly sliced

1 red pepper, deseeded and thinly sliced

55 g/2 oz raisins

85 g/3 oz butter

85 g/3 oz plain flour

850 ml/1½ pints milk

115 g/4 oz Cheddar cheese, grated

350 g/12 oz canned sweetcorn, drained

400 g/14 oz canned cannellini beans, drained and rinsed

2 tbsp chopped fresh parsley

4 egg yolks

salt and pepper

Beef & Spinach Cannelloni

1. Cook the spinach in just the water clinging to the leaves for 5–8 minutes, until tender, then drain and squeeze out as much liquid as possible. Chop finely.

2. Melt 15 g/½ oz of the butter with the oil in a large frying pan. Add the shallots and garlic and cook over a low heat, stirring occasionally, for 5 minutes, until softened. Add the beef, increase the heat to medium and cook, stirring frequently and breaking it up with a wooden spoon, for 8–10 minutes, until evenly browned. Add the spinach and cook for 3–4 minutes. Transfer the mixture to a bowl and stir in 3 tablespoons of the Parmesan, 1½ tablespoons of the cream, the egg and oregano. Season to taste with salt and pepper.

3. Preheat the oven to 190°C/375°F/Gas Mark 5. Melt 25 g/ 1 oz of the remaining butter in a saucepan, then stir in the flour and cook, stirring constantly, for 2 minutes. Remove the pan from the heat and gradually stir in the milk and the remaining cream, until smooth. Return the pan to the heat and bring to the boil, stirring constantly. Remove from the heat.

4. Fill the cannelloni tubes with the beef mixture. Pour a little of the tomato sauce over the base of an ovenproof dish, then put the cannelloni in the dish in two layers. Spoon the white sauce over them and top with the remaining tomato sauce. Sprinkle with the remaining Parmesan and dot with the remaining butter. Bake in the preheated oven for 30 minutes. Serve immediately.

Serves 4

175 g/6 oz spinach, coarse stalks removed
55 g/2 oz butter
1½ tbsp olive oil
2 shallots, finely chopped
2 garlic cloves, finely chopped
225 g/8 oz fresh beef mince
115 g/4 oz Parmesan cheese, finely grated
4½ tbsp double cream
1 egg, lightly beaten
pinch of dried oregano
4 tbsp plain flour
175 ml/6 fl oz milk
16 no pre-cook cannelloni tubes
1 quantity Tomato Sauce (see page 36)
salt and pepper

Spicy

Chilli Burgers

1. Preheat the grill. Mix together the onion, breadcrumbs, coriander, chilli powder, garlic salt, cumin and milk in a bowl. Add the beef and mix well with your hands until thoroughly combined.

2. Divide the mixture into four portions and shape into patties. Cook under the preheated grill for 5–8 minutes on each side, until cooked to your liking.

3. Spread the base of each bun with a little guacamole and top with the lettuce leaves, burgers and tomato slices. Cover with the tops of the buns. Serve immediately with tortilla chips.

Serves 4

1 small onion, finely chopped

55 g/2 oz fresh breadcrumbs

2 tbsp chopped fresh coriander

½ tsp chilli powder or cayenne pepper

½ tsp garlic salt

1 tsp ground cumin

100 ml/3½ fl oz milk

1 kg/2 lb 4 oz fresh beef mince

To serve
4 hamburger buns, split and toasted

guacamole

lettuce leaves

tomato slices

tortilla chips

Enchiladas

1. Heat 1 tablespoon of the oil in a frying pan. Add three quarters of the onions and half the garlic and cook over a low heat, stirring occasionally, for 5 minutes. Add the beef, increase the heat to medium and cook, stirring frequently and breaking it up with a wooden spoon, for 8–10 minutes, until evenly browned. Remove the pan from the heat and transfer the mixture to a bowl. Stir in the Cheddar cheese and three quarters of the chillies and season to taste with salt and pepper.

2. Heat the remaining oil in a saucepan. Add the remaining onion, garlic and chilli and cook over a medium heat, stirring occasionally, for 7–8 minutes. Stir in the tomatoes, tomato purée, oregano, Tabasco sauce and sugar, then season to taste with salt and cook for a further 3 minutes. Stir in the cream, then reduce the heat, cover and simmer, stirring occasionally, for 15 minutes. Remove from the heat and leave to cool slightly.

3. Meanwhile, preheat the oven to 180°C/350°F/Gas Mark 4. Heat a frying pan and brush with oil. One at a time, dip the tortillas in the tomato sauce, shake off any excess and cook for 30 seconds on each side. Transfer to a large plate, put a tablespoon of the beef mixture in the centre and roll up. Put the filled tortillas in a large ovenproof dish and pour the remaining tomato sauce over them. Sprinkle with the Parmesan and bake in the preheated oven for 15–20 minutes. Serve immediately.

Serves 6

4 tbsp corn oil, plus extra for brushing

2 onions, finely chopped

2 garlic cloves, finely chopped

225 g/8 oz fresh beef mince

55 g/2 oz Cheddar cheese, grated

4 fresh red chillies, deseeded and finely chopped

400 g/14 oz canned chopped tomatoes

115 g/4 oz tomato purée

pinch of dried oregano

dash of Tabasco sauce

1 tsp sugar

125 ml/4 fl oz double cream

18 flour tortillas or corn tortillas

2 tbsp grated Parmesan cheese

salt and pepper

33

Chilli con Carne

1. Heat the oil in a large saucepan. Add the onions and garlic and cook over a low heat, stirring occasionally, for 5 minutes, until softened. Add the beef, increase the heat to medium and cook, stirring frequently and breaking it up with a wooden spoon, for 8–10 minutes, until evenly browned.

2. Stir in the tomatoes, tomato purée, cumin, cayenne pepper, chilli powder, oregano, bay leaf and stock, then season to taste with salt and bring to the boil. Reduce the heat, cover and simmer, stirring occasionally, for 1 hour.

3. Add the kidney beans, re-cover the pan and simmer, stirring occasionally, for a further 30 minutes. Remove and discard the bay leaf and serve immediately with rice.

Serves 6

2 tbsp corn oil

2 onions, thinly sliced

2 garlic cloves, finely chopped

650 g/1 lb 7 oz fresh beef mince

200 g/7 oz canned chopped tomatoes

5 tbsp tomato purée

1 tsp ground cumin

1 tsp cayenne pepper

1 tbsp chilli powder

1 tsp dried oregano

1 bay leaf

350 ml/12 fl oz beef stock

400 g/14 oz canned red kidney beans, drained and rinsed

salt

cooked rice, to serve

34

Fiery Beef Tacos

1. Heat the oil in a frying pan. Add the onion and garlic and cook over a low heat, stirring occasionally, for 5 minutes, until softened. Add the beef, increase the heat to medium and cook, stirring frequently and breaking it up with a wooden spoon, for 8–10 minutes, until evenly browned. Drain off as much fat as possible.

2. Stir in the chilli powder and cumin, season to taste with salt and pepper and cook over a low heat, stirring frequently for a further 8 minutes, then remove from the heat.

3. Heat the taco shells according to the packet instructions. Meanwhile, peel, stone and slice the avocado and gently toss with the lemon juice in a bowl.

4. Divide the lettuce, spring onions, tomatoes and avocado slices among the taco shells. Add a tablespoon of soured cream to each, then divide the beef mixture among them. Sprinkle with the cheese and serve immediately.

Serves 4

2 tbsp corn oil

1 small onion, finely chopped

2 garlic cloves, finely chopped

280 g/10 oz fresh beef mince

1½ tsp hot chilli powder

1 tsp ground cumin

8 taco shells

1 avocado

2 tbsp lemon juice

¼ head of lettuce, shredded

4 spring onions, thinly sliced

2 tomatoes, peeled and diced

125 ml/4 fl oz soured cream

115 g/4 oz Cheddar cheese, grated

salt and pepper

35

Burritos

1. Soak the beans overnight in a bowl of cold water, then drain. Put the beans into a large saucepan and pour in water to cover. Bring to the boil and boil vigorously for 15 minutes, then drain and return to the pan. Add fresh water to cover and bring to the boil. Reduce the heat, cover and simmer for 1–1½ hours, until tender, then drain.

2. Heat the oil in a large saucepan. Add the onion, garlic and red pepper and cook over a low heat, stirring occasionally, for 5 minutes, until softened. Add the beef, increase the heat to medium and cook, stirring frequently and breaking it up with a wooden spoon, for 8–10 minutes, until evenly browned. Reduce the heat, stir in the spices, oregano and tomato ketchup and season to taste with salt. Add the wine, tomatoes, bay leaf and beans and mix well. Cover and simmer, stirring occasionally, for 25 minutes. Stir in the jalapeño chillies and coriander and remove from the heat. Remove and discard the bay leaf.

3. Meanwhile, preheat the oven to 180°C/350°F/Gas Mark 4. Brush a large ovenproof dish with oil. Using a slotted spoon, divide the meat mixture among the tortillas and roll up. Put them in the prepared dish, seam-side down, and sprinkle with the cheese. Bake in the preheated oven for 15 minutes. Serve immediately with the guacamole and salsa.

Serves 6

225 g/8 oz dried black beans

2 tbsp vegetable oil, plus extra for brushing

1 Spanish onion, chopped

2 garlic cloves, finely chopped

1 red pepper, deseeded and chopped

550 g/1 lb 4 oz fresh beef mince

1 tbsp ground cumin

1 tsp paprika

¼ tsp cayenne pepper

pinch of dried oregano

2 tbsp tomato ketchup

100 ml/3½ fl oz red wine

400 g/14 oz canned chopped tomatoes

1 bay leaf

3 tbsp chopped pickled jalapeño chillies

1 tbsp chopped fresh coriander

12 flour tortillas

70 g/2½ oz Cheddar cheese, grated

salt

guacamole and salsa, to serve

36

Empanadas

1. Heat the oil in a large frying pan. Add the onion, garlic and red pepper and cook over a low heat, stirring occasionally, for 5 minutes. Add the beef, increase the heat to medium and cook, stirring frequently and breaking it up with a wooden spoon, for 8–10 minutes, until evenly browned. Drain off as much fat as possible.

2. Stir the tomatoes, raisins, chilli powder and cumin into the pan, then season to taste with salt and pepper, reduce the heat and simmer for 10 minutes. Remove the pan from the heat.

3. Meanwhile, preheat the oven to 190°C/375°F/Gas Mark 5. Brush a large baking sheet with oil. Roll out the pastry on a lightly floured surface and stamp out eight rounds with a 13-cm/5-inch plain cutter. Put a tablespoon of the beef mixture on one side of each dough round, brush the edges with water and fold over. Press the edges with a fork or your finger to seal.

4. Transfer to the prepared baking sheet and bake in the preheated oven for 30–35 minutes, until golden brown. Serve immediately.

Makes 8

2 tbsp corn oil, plus extra for brushing

1 onion, finely chopped

1 garlic clove, finely chopped

½ small red pepper, deseeded and diced

225 g/8 oz fresh beef mince

2 tomatoes, peeled and diced

55 g/2 oz raisins

½–1 tsp chilli powder

pinch of ground cumin

300 g/10½ oz ready-made puff pastry, thawed if frozen

plain flour, for dusting

salt and pepper

Nachos

1. Preheat the oven to 180°C/350°F/Gas Mark 4. Heat the oil in a large frying pan. Add the onion and garlic, if using, and cook over a low heat, stirring occasionally, for 5 minutes, until softened. Add the beef, increase the heat to medium and cook, stirring frequently and breaking it up with a wooden spoon, for 8–10 minutes, until evenly browned. Remove from the heat, drain off as much fat as possible and season to taste with salt and pepper.

2. Spread out the tortilla chips in a large ovenproof dish and spoon the refried beans evenly over them. Sprinkle with half the cheese, cover with the beef mixture and sprinkle with the remaining cheese. Sprinkle with the jalapeño chillies and bake in the preheated oven for 10–15 minutes, until the cheese has melted. Serve immediately with soured cream, guacamole and salsa.

Serves 4–6

1 tbsp corn oil

1 onion, finely chopped

1 garlic clove, finely chopped (optional)

500 g/1 lb 2 oz fresh beef mince

450 g/1 lb tortilla chips

400 g/14 oz canned refried beans

225 g/8 oz Cheddar cheese, coarsely grated

4 tbsp chopped pickled jalapeño chillies

salt and pepper

soured cream, guacamole and salsa, to serve

Mexican Beef Stew

① Heat the oil in a large saucepan. Add the onion, garlic and green pepper and cook over a low heat, stirring occasionally, for 5 minutes. Add the beef, increase the heat to medium and cook, stirring frequently and breaking it up with a wooden spoon, for 8–10 minutes, until evenly browned.

② Stir in the chillies, cumin seeds, coriander, sweetcorn, kidney beans, tomato purée and stock, then season to taste with salt and pepper. Reduce the heat, cover and simmer, stirring occasionally, for 50–60 minutes. Serve immediately.

Serves 4

2 tbsp corn oil

1 onion, finely chopped

2 garlic cloves, finely chopped

1 green pepper, deseeded and finely chopped

500 g/1 lb 2 oz fresh beef mince

3 fresh green chillies, deseeded and finely chopped

1 tsp cumin seeds, lightly toasted

1 tbsp chopped fresh coriander

140 g/5 oz canned sweetcorn, drained

200 g/7 oz canned red kidney beans, drained and rinsed

1 tbsp tomato purée

450 ml/16 fl oz beef stock

salt and pepper

Beef Curry

1. Heat the oil in a frying pan. Add the onions, garlic and ginger and cook over a low heat, stirring occasionally, for 5 minutes, until softened. Add the ground coriander, chilli powder and turmeric and cook, stirring occasionally, for a further 3 minutes.

2. Add the beef, increase the heat to medium and cook, stirring frequently and breaking it up with a wooden spoon, for 8–10 minutes, until evenly browned. Stir in the tomatoes and season to taste with salt. Reduce the heat, cover and simmer, stirring occasionally, for 15 minutes. Uncover the pan and cook for a further 5 minutes.

3. Taste and adjust the seasoning, adding more salt if needed. Transfer the curry to a warmed serving dish, sprinkle with the chopped coriander and serve immediately with rice.

Serves 4

3 tbsp corn oil

4 onions, thinly sliced

2 garlic cloves, finely chopped

2.5-cm/1-inch piece fresh ginger, finely chopped

1 tsp ground coriander

1 tsp chilli powder

1 tsp ground turmeric

650 g/1 lb 7 oz fresh beef mince

200 g/7 oz canned chopped tomatoes

2 tbsp chopped fresh coriander

salt

cooked rice, to serve

Beef Samosas

1. For the dough, sift together the flour and salt into a bowl and make a well in the centre. Pour the oil into the well and add the water. Gradually incorporate the dry ingredients into the liquid, adding a little more water if necessary. Turn out onto a lightly floured surface and knead until smooth and elastic. Shape into a ball and leave to rest for 30 minutes.

2. Meanwhile, heat the oil in a large frying pan. Add the onion, garlic and ginger and cook over a low heat, stirring occasionally, for 5 minutes, until softened. Stir in the chilli powder, turmeric, ground coriander and garam masala and cook, stirring occasionally, for 3 minutes. Add the beef, increase the heat to medium and cook, stirring frequently and breaking it up with a wooden spoon, for 8–10 minutes, until evenly browned. Stir in the lemon juice and mint and leave to cool.

3. Divide the dough into 14 pieces. Roll out each piece into an oval about 20 cm/8 inches long, then cut in half widthways. Brush the straight edge of one piece with water and fold in each side to make a cone. Put a tablespoonful of the beef mixture into the cone, brush the open side with water and press to seal. Make 27 more samosas in the same way.

4. Heat enough oil for deep-frying in a deep-fat fryer to 180–190°C/350–375°F, or until a cube of bread browns in 30 seconds. Add the samosas, in batches, and cook until crisp and golden brown. Serve immediately with chilli sauce.

Makes 28

2 tbsp sunflower oil, plus extra for deep-frying
1 onion, chopped
2 garlic cloves, finely chopped
4-cm/1½-inch piece fresh ginger, grated
1 tsp chilli powder
1 tsp ground turmeric
1 tsp ground coriander
1 tsp garam masala
500 g/1 lb 2 oz fresh beef mince
juice of ½ lemon
3 tbsp chopped fresh mint
chilli sauce, to serve

Dough
225 g/8 oz plain flour, plus extra for dusting
large pinch of salt
2 tbsp sunflower oil
about 5 tbsp warm water

Special

41

Chinese Soup with Meatballs

1. Put the mushrooms into a bowl and pour in warm water to cover. Leave to soak for 15 minutes, then drain and squeeze dry. Discard the stalks and thinly slice the caps.

2. Mix together the beef, onion, garlic, cornflour and egg in a bowl until thoroughly combined. Shape the mixture into small balls, drop them into a bowl of iced water and leave to stand for 15 minutes.

3. Pour the stock into a large saucepan and bring to the boil. Drain the meatballs well, add to the pan and bring back to the boil. Reduce the heat and simmer for 10 minutes. Add the mushrooms, watercress, spring onions and soy sauce to taste and simmer for a further 2 minutes. Serve immediately.

Serves 4–6

5 dried Chinese mushrooms

350 g/12 oz fresh beef mince

1 onion, finely chopped

1 garlic clove, finely chopped

1 tbsp cornflour

1 egg, lightly beaten

850 ml/1½ pints beef stock

1 bunch of watercress (about 25 g/1 oz), stalks removed

3 spring onions, finely chopped

1–1½ tbsp soy sauce

42

Beef & Onion Piroshki

1. For the dough, sift the flour and salt into a bowl. Add the cream cheese and butter, then rub in with your fingertips until the mixture resembles breadcrumbs. Add 1 tablespoon of the water and mix in, then add 1 tablespoon of the cream and mix in. Repeat twice more. Knead gently, adding a little more water if necessary, then shape into a ball, cover and chill in the refrigerator for 30 minutes.

2. Meanwhile, melt the butter in a saucepan. Add the onion and cook over a low heat, stirring occasionally, for 5 minutes, until softened. Add the beef, increase the heat to medium and cook, stirring frequently and breaking it up with a wooden spoon, for 8–10 minutes, until evenly browned. Remove the pan from the heat, stir in the rice, soured cream, Worcestershire sauce, caraway seeds and chopped egg and season to taste with salt and pepper.

3. Preheat the oven to 200°C/400°F/Gas Mark 6. Grease two baking sheets with butter. Roll out the dough to a thickness of about 3 mm/⅛ inch on a lightly floured surface. Stamp out rounds with an 8-cm/3¼-inch plain cutter. Put a teaspoon of the filling on each round. Brush the edges of the rounds with beaten egg, then fold the dough over the filling and press the edges to seal. Crimp the edges with a fork. Place on the prepared baking sheets and brush with the remaining beaten egg. Bake in the preheated oven for 20 minutes, until golden brown. Serve immediately.

Makes 40–45

55 g/2 oz butter, plus extra
   for greasing
1 onion, finely chopped
225 g/8 oz fresh beef mince
55 g/2 oz cooked rice
2 tbsp soured cream
1 tsp Worcestershire sauce
1 tsp caraway seeds
1 hard-boiled egg, chopped
1 egg, beaten with 1 tsp water
salt and pepper

Dough
350 g/12 oz plain flour,
   plus extra for dusting
pinch of salt
55 g/2 oz cream cheese
115 g/4 oz butter
about 3 tbsp water
3 tbsp double cream

Beef Pilau

1. Heat 3 tablespoons of the oil in a saucepan. Add two thirds of the onions and two thirds of the garlic and cook over a low heat, stirring occasionally, for 5 minutes, until softened. Add the rice, ground cumin, turmeric and coriander and cook, stirring constantly, for 1 minute. Pour in the stock and bring to the boil. Stir well, reduce the heat, cover and simmer for 15–20 minutes, until the rice is tender and the liquid has been absorbed.

2. Meanwhile, put the remaining onion, remaining garlic, the beef, mace, cumin seeds and mint into a bowl. Season to taste with salt and pepper and mix well with your hands until thoroughly combined. Shape into walnut-sized balls.

3. Heat the remaining oil in a frying pan. Add the meatballs and cook over a medium heat, turning occasionally, for 6–8 minutes, until evenly browned and cooked through. Remove from the pan and drain on kitchen paper.

4. Remove the rice mixture from the heat and stir in the butter, then gently stir in the meatballs. Transfer to a warmed serving dish, garnish with coriander sprigs and serve immediately.

Serves 4–6

125 ml/4 fl oz olive oil
3 onions, finely chopped
3 garlic cloves, finely chopped
800 g/1 lb 12 oz long-grain rice
1 tsp ground cumin
1 tsp ground turmeric
1 tsp ground coriander
1.7 litres/3 pints beef stock
600 g/1 lb 5 oz fresh beef mince
pinch of ground mace
1 tsp cumin seeds
2 tbsp chopped fresh mint
115 g/4 oz butter
salt and pepper
fresh coriander sprigs, to garnish

Beef en Croûte

1. Preheat the oven to 180°C/350°F/Gas Mark 4. Grease a 650-g/1 lb 7-oz loaf tin with butter. Put the beef, onions, garlic, breadcrumbs, apples, mustard and parsley into a bowl and mix well. Beat one of the eggs with the stock and add to the bowl. Season to taste with salt and pepper and mix until combined.

2. Spoon the mixture into the prepared tin. Stand the tin in a roasting tin and pour in water to come about halfway up the sides. Bake in the preheated oven for 45 minutes. Remove from the oven and remove the loaf tin from the roasting tin. Cover with greaseproof paper, weigh down lightly with a couple of small food cans and leave to cool completely. Remove the cans and paper and turn out when cold.

3. Preheat the oven to 220°C/425°F/Gas Mark 7. Roll out the pastry on a lightly floured surface to a thickness of 3–5 mm/⅛–¼ inch. Put the meatloaf in the centre, brush the edges of the pastry with water and fold over to enclose the meat completely, trimming off any excess pastry. Put the parcel, seam-side down, on a baking sheet. Roll out the trimmings and use to make decorations. Brush with water and arrange on top of the parcel. Lightly beat the remaining egg and brush it over the parcel, then make 2–3 slits in the pastry.

4. Bake in the preheated oven for 35 minutes, until puffed up and golden brown. Reduce the oven temperature to 180°C/350°F/Gas Mark 4 and bake for a further 10 minutes. Serve immediately.

Serves 4

butter, for greasing

* 350 g/12 oz fresh beef mince
* 2 onions, finely chopped
* 1 garlic clove, finely chopped

55 g/2 oz fresh breadcrumbs

2 tart eating apples, peeled, cored and finely chopped

1 tbsp Dijon mustard

2 tbsp chopped fresh parsley

2 eggs

4 tbsp beef stock

300 g/10½ oz ready-made puff pastry, thawed if frozen

plain flour, for dusting

* salt and pepper

Italian Croquettes

1. Cook the rice in a large saucepan of salted boiling water for 15–20 minutes, until tender. Drain, rinse with boiling water and return to the pan. Stir in half the butter, the Parmesan and parsley. Spread out on a baking sheet and leave to cool.

2. Meanwhile, melt the remaining butter with the olive oil in a saucepan. Add the shallot and garlic and cook over a low heat, stirring occasionally, for 5 minutes, until softened. Add the beef, increase the heat to medium and cook, stirring frequently and breaking it up with a wooden spoon, for 5–8 minutes, until evenly browned. Stir in the wine and cook for 5 minutes. Reduce the heat and stir in the tomato purée, then cover and simmer for 15 minutes. Season to taste with salt and pepper and remove from the heat.

3. When the rice mixture is cold, shape it into balls about the size of a large egg and make a small hollow in each. Put a spoonful of meat mixture and a cube of cheese in each hollow, then re-shape to enclose the filling completely.

4. Lightly beat the eggs in a shallow dish and spread out the flour in a separate shallow dish. Dip the croquettes first in the egg and then in the flour to coat. Heat enough sunflower oil for deep-frying in a deep-fat fryer to 180–190°C/350–375°F, or until a cube of bread browns in 30 seconds. Add the croquettes, in batches, and fry until golden brown all over. Drain on kitchen paper and serve immediately.

Serves 4

300 g/10½ oz long-grain rice
55 g/2 oz butter
2 tbsp grated Parmesan cheese
1 tbsp chopped fresh parsley
1 tbsp olive oil
1 shallot, finely chopped
1 garlic clove, finely chopped
115 g/4 oz fresh beef mince
100 ml/3½ fl oz dry white wine
2 tbsp tomato purée
115 g/4 oz mozzarella cheese, cut into cubes
2 eggs
55 g/2 oz plain flour
sunflower oil, for deep-frying
salt and pepper

46

French Beef Patties in Red Wine

1. Melt 25 g/1 oz of the butter in a frying pan. Add the onions and garlic and cook over a low heat, stirring occasionally, for 5 minutes, until softened. Transfer the mixture to a bowl, add the beef, oregano, parsley and egg and season to taste with salt and pepper. Mix well with your hands until thoroughly combined.

2. Shape the mixture into four patties, each about 2 cm/¾ inch thick. Dust with the flour, gently shaking off the excess.

3. Melt half the remaining butter with the oil in a frying pan. Add the patties and cook for 3–4 minutes on each side, until cooked to your liking. Using a fish slice, transfer the patties to a serving dish and keep warm.

4. Pour off the fat from the frying pan, then add the wine and bring to the boil over a medium–high heat. Boil until reduced by about half. Meanwhile, dice the remaining butter. Remove the pan from the heat and whisk in the butter, one piece at a time, making sure each piece has been incorporated before adding the next. Pour the sauce over the patties, garnish with parsley and serve immediately.

Serves 4

- 85 g/3 oz butter
- 2 red onions, finely chopped
- 1 garlic clove, finely chopped
- 650 g/1 lb 7 oz fresh beef mince
- ½ tsp dried oregano
- 1 tbsp chopped fresh parsley, plus extra to garnish
- 1 egg, lightly beaten
- 55 g/2 oz plain flour
- 1 tbsp olive oil
- 150 ml/5 fl oz red wine
- salt and pepper

47

Lemon Beef in Walnut Sauce

1. Tear the bread into pieces, put it into a large bowl with the milk and leave to soak for 5 minutes. Add the beef, garlic, lemon rind and egg, season to taste with salt and pepper and mix well until thoroughly combined. Using your hands, shape pieces of the mixture into walnut-sized balls.

2. Melt 55 g/2 oz of the butter in a frying pan. Add the meatballs, in batches, and cook over a medium heat, turning frequently, for 5 minutes, until browned all over. Remove with a slotted spoon.

3. Melt the remaining butter in a large saucepan. Add the onions and cook over a low heat, stirring occasionally, for 5 minutes, until softened. Add the walnuts and cook, stirring frequently, for a further 5 minutes. Pour in the water and bring to the boil. Add the pomegranate juice, lemon juice and sugar, then season to taste with salt and pepper. Reduce the heat and simmer, stirring frequently, for 30 minutes.

4. Add the meatballs to the saucepan and simmer very gently for 1½ hours, until almost all the liquid has been absorbed. Transfer to a warmed serving dish, garnish with strips of lemon zest and serve immediately.

Serves 4

1 slice white bread, crusts removed

2 tbsp milk

500 g/1 lb 2 oz fresh beef mince

1 garlic clove, finely chopped

1 tbsp finely grated lemon rind

1 egg, lightly beaten

85 g/3 oz butter

3 onions, finely chopped

140 g/5 oz walnuts, finely chopped

600 ml/1 pint water

5 tbsp pomegranate juice

1 tbsp lemon juice

1½ tbsp sugar

salt and pepper

strips of lemon zest, to garnish

48

Beef with Red Pepper, Fruit & Nuts

1. Heat the oil in a large frying pan. Add the onions, garlic, celery and red pepper and cook over a low heat, stirring occasionally, for 5 minutes. Add the beef, increase the heat to medium and cook, stirring frequently and breaking it up with a wooden spoon, for 8–10 minutes, until evenly browned.

2. Add the tomatoes, haricot beans, tomato purée, chilli powder, nutmeg, apples, apricots, almonds and French beans. Season to taste with salt and pepper. Reduce the heat, cover and simmer for 30 minutes, then remove the lid and simmer for a further 10 minutes. Serve immediately, garnished with slivered almonds.

Serves 4

3 tbsp sunflower oil

2 onions, finely chopped

2 garlic cloves, finely chopped

2 celery sticks, chopped

1 red pepper, deseeded and chopped

1 kg/2 lb 4 oz fresh beef mince

400 g/14 oz canned chopped tomatoes

400 g/14 oz canned haricot beans, drained and rinsed

6 tbsp tomato purée

1 tsp chilli powder

½ tsp ground nutmeg

2 tart eating apples, cored and chopped

55 g/2 oz ready-to-eat dried apricots, chopped

2 tbsp slivered almonds, plus extra to garnish

115 g/4 oz frozen French beans, thawed

salt and pepper

49

Minced Beef Stroganoff

1. Heat 2 tablespoons of the oil in large frying pan. Add the onion and garlic and cook over a low heat, stirring occasionally, for 5 minutes, until softened. Add the mushrooms and cook, stirring frequently, for a further 5 minutes. Using a slotted spoon, transfer the vegetables to a plate.

2. Add the remaining oil to the pan, then add the beef and cook over a medium heat, stirring frequently and breaking it up with a wooden spoon, for 5–8 minutes, until evenly browned. Drain off as much fat as possible.

3. Reduce the heat to low, return the vegetables to the pan and stir in the brandy. Cook, stirring occasionally, for 4–5 minutes, until the alcohol has evaporated. Stir in the stock, season to taste with salt and pepper and simmer gently, stirring frequently, for 15 minutes.

4. Stir in the soured cream and parsley and cook for a further minute. Garnish with parsley and serve immediately.

Serves 4

3 tbsp sunflower oil

1 onion, chopped

2 garlic cloves, finely chopped

225 g/8 oz mushrooms, sliced

500 g/1 lb 2 oz fresh beef mince

2 tbsp brandy

150 ml/5 fl oz beef stock

150 ml/5 fl oz soured cream

2 tbsp chopped fresh parsley, plus extra to garnish

salt and pepper

50

Chinese Noodles with Beef & Shredded Vegetables

1. Put the beansprouts and shredded vegetables into small serving dishes and set aside. Cook the noodles in a large pan of salted boiling water according to the packet instructions, then drain and keep warm.

2. Meanwhile, heat a wok over a medium heat, then add the groundnut oil and swirl it around the pan to heat. Add the spring onions, garlic and ginger and stir-fry for 2 minutes. Add the beef and stir-fry, breaking it up with a wooden spoon, for 5 minutes, until evenly browned. Stir in the sesame oil, soy sauce, rice wine and sugar and cook, stirring constantly, for a further 3 minutes.

3. Mix the cornflour to a paste with the water in a small bowl and add to the wok. Simmer, stirring constantly, until the sauce has thickened and become glossy.

4. Divide the noodles among individual bowls and top with the beef mixture and shredded vegetables. Serve immediately.

Serves 4–6

500 g/1 lb 2 oz dried egg noodles

3 tbsp groundnut oil

3 spring onions, thinly sliced

2 garlic cloves, finely chopped

1-cm/½-inch piece fresh ginger, finely chopped

350 g/12 oz fresh beef mince

1 tbsp sesame oil

5 tbsp soy sauce

2 tbsp Chinese rice wine or dry sherry

1 tbsp sugar

1 tbsp cornflour

4 tbsp water

salt

To serve

115 g/4 oz fresh beansprouts, blanched

115g/4 oz Chinese leaves, blanched and shredded

115 g/4 oz carrots, blanched and shredded

115 g/4 oz cucumber, shredded

115 g/4 oz radishes, shredded